beyond the brokenness

Evelyn McKellar

BookLeaf Publishing

Presentation by *BookLeaf Publishing*

Web: www.bookleafpub.com

E-mail: info@bookleafpub.com

ISBN: 9789357690737

First edition 2022

For Stephanie

.fresh.

Overdosing on uncertainty
the unknown ahead
like fresh snow
clean white
used to stir you
excited
delighted.
Now, nervous system on overdrive
more flighted,
than a 737.

Used to chart courses where
others' tracks had tread
follow in their stead
for the wisdom of the world
now the insight and advice unfurled
leaves us curled
in fetal position
searching for meaningful
trustworthy premonition
choking down new variant admonition,
In this condition:
languishing.

Tangled
strangled
hope feels dangled
mental health mangled
choking on unbridled possibility.
Cancellations,
vaccinations,
protests and political degradations,
this imbalance has heightened agitations,
exposed societal gaps
and racist infestations,
impact felt for generations,
across screens you steward communal congratulations,
locked in echo chamber salutations,
each wave makes pointless any social reservations.

Inhale.

Exhale.

Snow falls
as winter calls
great pause gives awes
and a chance to soften our clenched jaws.
Step forward into the fresh blanket
path yet unsighted
steady the steps

who bring foundation to the heart.
As you start
snow beckons the going slow
as the world feels like it's burning
but continues turning
you look back
bear witness to the tracks
made by your intention,
insight crafts premonition
heed the careful admonition
look lovingly on the other with contrition
release the stifling fear-led superstition
and try to listen
to that inward vision.
Perhaps we break free from inward prison
as the fresh snow glistens
so may a new hopeful, healthy dawn
no longer be hidden.

.hypervigilance.

Insistent upon keeping you safe
fear reminds from
behind you
hide you
from all that might injure.

Grinding
your soul into a pocket size, carry-on
so no one can discover
the valuable you're packing
fear narratives are stacking
as your back starts cracking.
Too much weight
fearing so many
disastrous
potential fates
in this state.

Can you relate?

In this state,
love deflates
like an air pocket
caught outside the lung lining
crushing breath of life

with self-stifling injections,
protections from anticipated strife.

Robbed of joy
hyper-vigilance keeps you
at the ready
perpetually unsteady.
Forces engaged
prepared to deploy
the narratives they employ
masked as "wisdom"
they seek to destroy
any perceived threats
so you can live with zero regrets
yet on further inspect
living wholeheartedly becomes the discarded
reject.

You thought securing
all the right features
would be all the needed teachers,
but life can't be lived from the bleachers.

Joy, if we listen,
beseecher invites
excites
step out from the hiding
and into the (de)light.
Carry with you the fright

as it shudders and cringes.
Companion it
as it worries
you've come off your hinges.

Employ its protection,
with compassion, re-direction
at joy's discretion
let fear come alongside
and give discernment
to the adventurous ride.
Fear will see
safety is not purely, securely
protected
when you hide;
even if it hurts
life is meant to be taken in stride.

Go with healing introspection
release the tools of deflection,
and amidst
loving connection,
abide.

.containers.

I used to dream
in cages,
prewritten were all the pages;
my imagination soared
only as wide as the painted walls around me.

If imagination dared
to dream wider than the edges
to nurture visions from soulful
dredges,
quickly emerged
manicured hedges.
Inner Light obscured
by carefully crafted tradition
beating the imagination into defeated
submission;
eventually dreaming falls to attrition.

Acceptance from the collective
offered allure
belonging ensured
by falling in line
hedges designed
to subdue the more soulful mind.

I used to dream in cages,
surprised by my rages
that shook the halls
made blinders fall
until cracks in the walls
let in whispers, from sages;
invitations to explore
beyond the prewritten pages.
Insight came in subtle,
felt sense,
unable-to-fully-fit-in-and-sit-still
stages.

Glimmers of insight
from agitated mind
wrestled open the unspoken radiant design.
Reflection invited remind
of wide open spaces
that once allowed dreams
to fill and play.

Turns out
the hedging
caging walls
arose slowly, in dismay.
An understandable way,
trying to allay
pain and neglect
deeper inspect

discovered confused and cold reject
protection
from dismantling responses
dreams fled into obscurity
bargaining for security.

But once awake
to the yearnings of the soul
no longer content to pass time
until we are old
a deeper sense of need unfolds.
Awakening may incur the collective to scold;
true-to-self might mean the cage's welcome is
cold.

Bold
is the heart releasing the need to belong
who nurtures with clarity a deeper song
who is willing to be wrong
in the eyes of the cage
who is willing to honor
what's beneath the rage.
Soon the awake heart
finds the body to be a sage
enraged and alive
she must pursue more than merely survive.

I used to dream in cages
but in stages

container crumbled
footsteps upon the prescribed treadmill for life's
"shoulds" fumbled
the imagination and awake soul stumbled
out of sight of the collective
into the light and self-directive
from now on introspective
reflective
attentive.

Where we go there may be no roads
goads pierce
from those who are still painting cages,
but as you trudge and step and stumble and
explore
despite feeling misunderstood and deplored,
no "best" from before
replaces
the soulfully found ground
reverberating in naturally aligned spaces
no longer held by "should" ingratiating;
caged narratives found to be emaciating.

Be not dismayed at the lack of a map
or the widening gap
between you and the collective
belonging now to life's rhythms and light
released from image maintenance and guided by
inner sight.

Take notice
at this table laid daily by breath
a savory essence
light that defies
daily dissociative
death.
Be not bereft
at the group mind you've left.
Nimble and deft
is the soul as navigator
honoring breath and body:
a better teacher than the caged and burnt out
preacher.

I used to dream in cages
shaken loose by deep soul rages.
In stages
awaken
through breath to reach her:
the soulful inner teacher.
Clever guide within the dark
inner compass seeks what's true
good
beautiful
alive
striving for beyond the caged idea to survive.
Tread soulfully for what it means for you to
thrive.

.grip.

Shame tackles me
like I've stolen technology
and I'm running out the door
floored.
If someone's keeping score
I'm losing
against
me.
Or it sounds like me.
But it can't be.
Surely
me
isn't this mean, cruel, dark, unkind?
Rewind.

She's my slave driver
am I the cart or the horse?
Overdriven.

Shame's a dam
and I'm the levee breaking
shaking
energy quaking
hopefully in therapy

remaking
healthier paths.

She buries me,
drowning current carries me
away from all the love.

She’s a weighted blanket
and the rebuttals keep piling on the weight.

.leaves released.

I want my people
pleasing
postures and
practices
to fall like the leaves
from these autumnal trees.
May the green that once thrived
of my survival instincts
subside
wither up and die
become parched and starved
for the affirming self-dis-serving nourishment
I'm accustomed to drinking in
thirsty for worthy
now choking on the lack of audience confirming
yearning for returning to that ever changing soil.
Clamoring with subservience to the social toil,
norms and expectations that
inform and guide my affectations
inclinations
limited stipulations
self-abandoned appropriations.

As leaves change their colors
to rosy and warm hues

affected by reduced nutrients
may the invitation of reduced
socially affirming subsistence
reach me
teach me to refuse to choose
someone else's praise
as confirmation of my identification.

Leaves in fiery colors cascade
as an empty tree is made
winter's arrival beckons grounded survival.
Finally, unburdened by the archival:
"who I should be?"

In winter, the lone tree is free
of last season
of other's reason
expectation's leaves left
the only things a tree needs:
to deeply abundantly be.

.threads.

You walked so long
with the aim to be strong
buried your song;
praised most for getting along.

Carried the pivoting
pretended the bullshit was riveting
as you danced through
the weight of getting smaller and smaller.

Hold all the threads
lest something precious be dead
never revealing:
it's your precious time
their productivity propaganda is stealing.
Shatter the ceiling,
embrace where your weary body is feeling
release the threads
that make you feel dead
and instead
step with ease and slowness;
reveal healing.

You walked so long
weary
teary
feary
carrying so many threads
trying not to drop anything
forget anything;
YOLO don’t miss anything.

Culture shifting
towards health we’re drifting
false narratives sifting.

You walked so long
with the heaviest pack
upon your back
prepared
led by “scared”
“just in case” an overstuffed weight to bear.

Dragging uphill and across many miles
every prepared context of
appropriate smiles
sensing but self-neglecting
unhealthy guiles.
All the whiles
back to back trials
led you growing
but not always showing:

this weight is breaking you down.
Are there any humans around?
Or is your limited capacity
a social and appropriate-ness travesty?
Submit to your majesty:
Protestant's work ethic has a hidden gravity.

Ankles ached
as spirit beneath the weight
buckled
Capitalism chuckled
at the farce they've convinced you is true.

But some have begun
doing the work
a new tapestry they spun
outgrew
all that you thought you knew:
what to carry
how to tarry
about who and when and why to marry.
So, despite the unknown
now we ferry
into unknown waters
uncharted sea
take time to know it's okay just to be;
trying to root instead into what it means
to be free.

.held.

When the weight on the shoulders
and the ache in the heart
the churning of the gut
and the sense that without me things will fall
apart
I start
to collapse
acknowledge the mental traps
and perhaps
if I'm wise to the lies disguised in
Capitalism's guise
I'll try
to let even my feet off the hook
with a rest
in my hammock
laying free in the sun
holding
for a moment
nothing up
except my gaze to the sky
reminded by the birds
that flying is often about letting the wind carry
you.

.womxn.

For what makes you, you
each day rising and more true
self-chosen
with each step unfrozen
as you are set free of what binds
and remind
this aching, weary world
for the millionth time
it is not the tomb
but the womb
making room.
Patriarchy keeps trying to exhume
old mechanisms of literalization,
infatuation
with a rigid, un-evolved inculturation.
If only,
as they dug in the ground,
dirt beneath their fingernails,
they could tune into the sound
of how life grows
in cycles
seasonal
rhythm and rebirth
beginning to unearth

life's balance and sacred feminine worth.
For you,
womxn in all shapes and form,
creativity
compassion
collaboration is your norm.
Healing nurtured in harmony,
for climate and policy.
Trust the wisdom of the breast,
a brilliant ecosystem and test
of rhythm responsive to need
creating what feeds
nurturing so that life may breathe.

For you,
where you have chosen to invest,
for the wisdom with which you release
and prioritize rest.

For you,
getting what has been suppressed
off your chest.
May your voice not be dismissed as mere jest.

For you,
celebrating,
re-calibrating,
partnering or solo-ing,

tiny humans raising,
business-creating,
degree obtaining,
retirement awaiting.

For you,
getting through,
uncovering,
re-mothering,
discovering:
the feminine self is desperately needed
so that we might know as kin
those we've too long been othering.

May there be more of the feminine
societal quaking,
dogma-shaking,
patriarchy-forsaking,
inclusion-making
postures,
as the feminine soul
wrest free from narrow-minded control -
colonial domination was never a worthy goal -
as more and more
learn to trust their wobbly feet
like the newborn foal.
I swear to God,
especially womxn were meant to read

that sacred scroll.
See all expressions, identities, and designations
bear the heart and strength in that stole.

Let womxn lead us into becoming whole.

.(en)force.

"Mary Shelley's warning rises from the story
sonorous and clear as larksong:
Life is not to be made,
unless it can be tended with love —
or else it dooms all involved
to a living death."
- The Marginalian

You celebrate with vigor
the 'freedom for the unborn'.
Protection, after
decades sought judicial redirection
never mind advancements in health care
grounded in evidence-based inspection;
all part of the 'liberal infection'.

Oppression
to the womb
preventing the fetus
from becoming entombed,
pro-life claims,
despite the post-womb life it maims
attempting to make culture -
via the female body -

more religiously tame.
Failing to protect the
41st week of life
from preventable systemic strife.
Let black and brown bodies stumble into gaps,
and sustainable protections lapse.

Why have we relapsed?
Five decades swiftly undone.
Fervent for the fetus yet
fail the children by NRA design;
this lobby more hospitable
to prioritizing the bottom line.

Religious-led,
faithfully proud,
'Making America racist' out loud.
You cry for birth to be required;
are you sure the result is what you desire?
Protections in this land
tend to expire.
You stand for the unborn
yet leave the lifecycle torn.
Pulverized by poverty
divvied by Jim Crow
the birth you enforce
leaving the hosting life shorn
forlorn and scorned,

for struggling to care for
that which you forced
from her womb to her hands
now resent her for the demands.

This system values profit over people
insurance plans more limiting than lenient
claims Jesus-loving
but the incarnation is inconvenient.

Can we acknowledge
life is beyond the 9 months you cherish;
force wombs to host and open
yet let life prematurely perish?
Life deserves to be stewarded
in a pipeline of care
not delivered into forgotten depths
not redlined into generational despair.

We can prepare,
via policy we can care;
holistic systems
releasing the greed
we can align with our environment
better steward the community in need.

Yes, life is deeply worthy;
let it also be sustainably sturdy:

health supported
communities connected
let the religion you love
leave no born body unprotected.

.anesthetize.

Anesthetized
hidden soul behind
cold, absent eyes
economics must despise
and want the demise
of our flesh and blood.
At this rate,
no rescue from the flood
that surrounds
and drowns us
indebted to the frenetic pace
so that as our hearts race
blood pressure to the skies
hypertension in our vessels and traumatic cries;
capitalism feeds us lies.

Work harder
and you'll reach the top.
Except the reality is our bodies never get to stop.
Only in heart and
organ system failure
we eventually drop;
never mind it was the wrong systems
that needed to be failing
while our bodies are flailing.

Anesthetized we stare at screens,
expensive money on face creams
dopamine scrolling
to ignore how we are being shredded at the
self-actualizing seams.

I stare at screens instead of you
heartache sometimes the only
force potent enough to
bring the present into view.
Can we re-sensitize so
it doesn't take our attention
so long to stew?
Let the organic soil beneath our feet
give us renew.

Environmental
true health is dealt
eco-systemical
circumstantial
satisfactual
gatekept for the
well off financial;
health shouldn't be only for one with wealth.

.prayer fragments.

Speaking of prayer
fragmented releases
pleases
give us eases
prostrated appeases
cure diseases…
where's Jesus?

Is our divine
an anchor
or
alighting
or
alignment?
Church organization can pander for the sacred
consignment:
treadmill of disconnected self-refinement
wondering why we feel
flawed
by designed intent.

We lift our lament
beg for the worthiness
feeling unsturdiness
unsteady

overstimulated by triggered nerviness.
Eventually the narrative
neglected nerves break down
health designs a flawed system to fracture
that enlightenment might rapture.
Wisdom starts to capture
tingles our senses
inhaling sustainability
deepened sense of virility
potential pangs of hostility as
old narratives crumble
system steps away from our fumble
prayers deflate to weary mumble
prostrate to
irate to
stepping willingly to own life's plate.

When will we inhale
the gift of this existence
drop shame's misguided insistence
unfollow
to inspect with thoughtful resistance.

I digress
for the sake of a rhyme.
Divine good
worth its salt
won't punish or pivot on a dime.

.illuminate the senses.

Smoke hangs in the air
like fog, yet
unfamiliar.
Obscurity here is different
this season:
not the density of moisture but
a lack of clean and clear air.

This season,
life's guidance and sense of self
obscured
beneath learning
orienting
adjusting
arriving
releasing old cultural narratives
and poor, cruel teachers
safe to sit humbly
at the feet of wiser experience
honest about feel
trusting that in due time
skills and wisdom will reveal.

When the air we breathe
and scenes we survey are obscure

how do we take in new ways of listening
navigate and steward
what we feel and sense and know?

Instead of understanding,
sensing;
integrated self-directed
sensation inspecting.

Ahead obscured,
no depth visible to the path ahead,
out of runway,
out of specific goals
with present arrival,
grounded
this is where you wanted to be.

This is you as you wanted to see and be seen.
And there are still disappointments
moments where it isn't making you feel happy
it's sad
or annoying
need to determine a boundary
but instead of moving forward
or walking away,
instead of an outward path
in this smokey fog
an inward one develops,
and like the pacific northwestern sky

feels all enveloping.
You walk in your life
working and learning
busy and frenetic
and then in some moments you come back
to sit
reflect
chew
sense
explore
inwardly.
What's moving?
What's inviting?
What's guiding?
Still propensity to look outward
but inward,
inward has become the path
like the smoke
foggy sibling
the view is obscured
because of the need to reconnect with this
inward one
obscurity a gift to the eyes
so that deeper insight might alight
illuminate
speculate inward.

.wagons in the sky.

Adventures in a childhood wagon
a stroll with beloved parent
pulled along in glee
carted and together
an adventure started.

Instead,
lines and drips
rates and pumps
weary
calm
young eyes
rest in the wagon
strolled across the bridge in the sky.
An afternoon walk
medical care cascading above
echoing,
harbinger of risk and childhood missed.
A mother's persistent steps
providing a soothing rest
for her little dove
meant to be flying
running
scampering
in this rainy clouded sky

instead of depleted rest in
wagon's weariness.
No doubt their journey has been bathed in
tearfulness.

Outside the rain falls
as a storm raging
mirroring the inner one
waging
in this sky and wagon's care
a battle for your health is staging
more experience than a kid should have with
doctor paging;
too much on the body can leave one
disengaging.

We, your neighbors on this bridge
companions in your adventure
masked
badged
to and from our health care tasks
minding the ecosystem of your care
hopefully,
staying aware
hopefully,
you find us and those you need
presently and lovingly there.

Along this bridge and the sky
we pace
with our masks
to our tasks
while in your wagon
a tortoise's race.
I suspect all a parent asks
is that their child would soon return to the
support of their legs
their unattached lines
their playful jubilant energy
their own embodied place against the raging and
alive sky.

Rest deeply,
little traveler.
In steadfast care
of the one stewarding your wagon's rest.
May this road in the sky
keep rising to meet you,
may the air up here release weight from
your chest
and may all of your cells
veins
and organs
be deeply and carefully
substantially and financially
irrevocably and inextricably
blessed.

.dear naivete.

Don't give up.
You may be holding your breath
or hiding beneath the cover of humility in the learning process,
but you are part of the fuel and strength,
enjoying the good and beautiful in people.

I see you exhale
at the end of the day
where all the learning
and not knowing
has taken away your play.
I know the last few years have taken your confidence away.
I see you
defeated and weary,
less cheery,
leery.
Time to engage.

You are a gift
unbridled by the raw and abrasive cynicism so many others bear.

You'll get there
little one,
keep breathing.
If you need to, keep hiding.
Let go of forces deriding
and chiding
you'll get their wisdom behind you and soon
be flying.
Your heart is needed
on the other side of this steep learning curve.
Hold fast;
your heart is most deserved.

.play poetry.

Let it be bad
unrhymed
ill-timed
feel silly and un-clever;
with your voice, endeavor.

Let it be new
stumbling and clunky like learning to walk;
know that this process too
is deeply adorable
not as deplorable
as we tend to think about ourselves
when we're adults.

All grown up and so serious
forgetting that life
started out playful
exploratory
invitational
imaginational;
this imperfect learning was sensational.

So let it be bad.
Let the unfiltered
raw

expression come out:
raging mad and collapsingly sad.
Let despair bleed onto the page
and joy release timidity
breaking free from proper's cage.

Let the abundance of you
spill out onto the page.

It's crucial
you hear you
all of you;
let wholeness enter the stage.

.taper.

You stare
at new walls
blank
possibility abounds
with tearful pause, you
blink
trying not to sink, into
unanticipated space;
what is absent is not yet replaced.

So many pictures
no longer accurate fixtures
held safely in boxes;
a story you'll no longer display.

Dismay, to discover
they are no longer on board
cut the cord
can't afford
to keep trying and vying
loose ends of unraveling
now need tying
sighing
exhale and inhale
trying not to faint

staring at new walls
awaiting fresh paint.

Their possibility
a metaphor.
Their blankness
an invitation.
Grief lays bare
what you thought would always be your
situation.
Blank walls,
empty shelves,
make space for
remaking ourselves.
As old seasons
torn out from under;
toss the story you thought you'd live asunder.

Your efforts and tries
earnest as they were
nver enough to convince
someone who wants out
to dig in, devout.

You may wonder
what lies beyond this grief:
a foggy barrier reef
wakes mysterious a formerly firm

seemingly secure
belief.

To the wayside
explanations fall
staring at blank walls
silence hovers over as a pall.
A whisper chokes thru heavy tears.
Inhale,
exhale,
breathing down.
Silence hangs
and drapes the moment
without a sound.
Inwardly,
a type of ground
is found.

The wave that washed
comes and goes
parasympathetic breathing slows
a deep and grounded voice
somehow knows.

New walls sing
unspoken potential
bend a deferential bow to
the builder
the painter

the artist
the chef
the author
the runner
to one who feels left.

Demure
unsure
this moment
may be
but see, and
be not mistaken;
something within you cannot be taken.

As you gaze at these walls
breathe and go slow
what is love will never fail to flow
in new forms and new spaces
in new chapters and new faces.
Within you,
there's ground.
Ahead of you
more life to be found.
Around you
grace abounds.

You stare
at new walls
blank

possibility abounds.
With tearful pause,
blink
breathe
know:
this ship will not sink.
Blank walls
abound with empty space
this canvas invites your
compassionate and creative embrace.

.near not yet.

Standing beside myself
wanting to re-inhabit
re-ignite
re-turn
to be integrated, I yearn.
Stand tall even when the feedback feels stern.
Or is my direction the bow?
Tip my brow
confidence tumbles
words fumble
questions stumble
in the growing and learning I trip
keep a firm grip
on my sense of self
confidence
and capability;
my faith shakes with instability
lacking foundation
history of learning without civility
my self-criticism has demonstrated virility
masquerading as humility
postures left me collapsing
in doubt of my ability.

Does the re-alignment come with the process?
Or am I relegated to disjointed confinement
until release results from resignment?
Can my hyper vigilance find reassignment?
Can confidence grow from knowing my gut,
trusting I am as the design meant?

Time will tell,
hope whispers in wondering
anticipating as I walk the road
this path leads towards self-refinement,
health
and grounded alignment.
Facing this obscured path forward
and inward is
in fact,
the healing assignment.

.show me your hard days.

Show me
the way you
hide the soft tears
or let them pour down
like a long-awaited rain after a drought
emptying you out
of the heartache.

Show me
the moments you
struggle to know
if what you're doing is the right path
or just the one you've invested the most time in.

Show me
how you make sense
of the laments and limits of this life,
hold hands with your days
when you're tired of believing
it is worthwhile to keep working.

Show me
how you hold the unanswerable questions
and keep taking care of the mundane.

Show me
how you turn on the same show to numb out
or cry yourself to sleep to a meditation podcast
bravely awaken the next morning
and pour yourself another cup of coffee and the
same cereal.

Show me
how you smile at your loved ones
and self in the mirror
again and again
after our system keeps trying to mold you into
machine
and neglect your humanity.

Show me
the collapses between the beautiful moments
the discouragements between the gratefuls
the whole spectrum of feelings
that must be running through you as it is me
in this work of being human.

Show me
your hard days
so I might know
in mine
that I'm not broken.

.stones at chimayo.

Spanish farmers
reposition stones in a riverbed
redirecting the flow
aiding the river
mindful of storm or drought
so that in those events
their village will never be without.

Every day
repositioning
each day
listening
to the work that needs to be done
following the water
clearing out
what prevents the flow of life
traveling down its intended -
unblock the distended -
path.

Every day
someone
somewhere
paints
some portion

of the San Francisco
Golden Gate Bridge,
a daily ritual of maintenance
that honors the gravity of time
and habitual layers of grime
that can cover us slowly
layers and barriers
grow without notice
until we cannot tell which way the water once flowed
until the bridge begins to rust and dwindle in structural integrity.

Every day,
I arrive to you
embracing that you will always be brand new
arriving to myself
as I become
and unwind
from the ways culture has taught me to mind.
It is connection
that guides my direction
community invites inner reflection
of the stones that block
our paths to one another.

The daily movement of stones
re-mends our inner status of soul and bones
daily committing to learning the path

between us.
Our connections take work.
Our nourishment takes work.
We can find ourselves so far from where we'd
like to be
individually
and even together.

So no matter the weather
we repair
arrive aware
taking great and precise care
to meet our path
and daily
remove the barriers
that prevent the flow of love.
After all,
Rumi reminds
our task is to seek and find
the stony barriers we've built against
love.

Peace
is release
a daily decrease
of cortisol elevation
breathe steadily in meditation
so that with less hesitation
we might receive

the every day
love and grace that ever flows our way.
It is in these daily
ritualized
practices of peace
that we pray
trying to stay
in the ever present current
between us.

Peace is the willingness
to move the first stone
to let no one journey alone
to find our way
internally
eternally
so that life may flow thoroughly
home.

www.ingramcontent.com/pod-product-compliance
Lightning Source LLC
Chambersburg PA
CBHW062202160726
48282CB00027B/963

9789357690737